The Secrets Of Good Parenting

How To Raise Happy Healthy And Successful Kids

Dr. Stella Reynolds

Table of Contents

Introduction

This book is a heartfelt conversation, a shared cup of wisdom steeped in experience, poured out with a genuine desire to empower you on your unique parenting odyssey.

As parents, we're all a work in progress, stumbling through the maze of raising resilient, compassionate, and successful individuals.

Prepare to discover the delicate dance between nurturing and letting go, the alchemy of instilling values while fostering independence. We'll explore the science of smiles, the art of effective communication, and the magic that happens when you embrace the messy, beautiful chaos of family life.

Join me in creating a nurturing environment where laughter echoes, dreams take flight, and every hug feels like home. The adventure begins now, and the destination is a future where your children thrive, and you flourish as a parent.

Chapter 1

Overcoming Fears And Embracing The Adventure Of Parenthood

The most thrilling, confusing, and downright amusing adventure life has to offer is being a parent. It's quite typical to experience a range of feelings as you approach the birth of your first child, from enthusiasm to anxiety.

But hey, what do you know? This is something you can handle! We'll talk about how to overcome your fear of the unknown and why you might want to have additional children in the future in this enjoyable parenting adventure.

The Great Unknown

Imagine having a map that is always updating as you get ready to travel to a place you have never been. Parenthood feels like that, and that's acceptable! There is no one-size-fits-all guidebook and no one person with all the answers. But the pleasure of discovery is in this immense unknown. Your child will impart knowledge to you that you never would have imagined, such as the importance of always watching over crayons or the reasons why "I can do it myself!" will become their catchphrase.

First Steps and Errors

The moment your child takes their first unsteady steps is captured in time. You will always be afraid to fall, but keep in mind that each stumble brings you one step closer to becoming a skilled balancer.

These little victories fill life, and before you know it, your youngster will be jumping around with delight.

Laughing like a baby The Best Medicine

Being a parent is similar to being an audience member at a comedy show when your child is the star. Kids can bring unadulterated humor into your life which is priceless. The show "Kids Say the Darndest Things" releases a new episode every day, complete with unexpected queries and mispronunciations. Even during the messiest of diaper changes, you'll be able to smile because of these memories.

Sweet Dreams and Sleepless Nights

Let's face it: becoming a parent at a young age sometimes involves sleep deprivation. You could be asking yourself, "Will I ever sleep again?" after those restless nights. But when your child goes to sleep and you cuddle with them, you'll find that the restless evenings are well worth it for the wonderful dreams they bring into your life.

First Words, First Hugs, and All Points In Between

Moments like your child's first "I love you" and when they put their little arms around you are priceless.

Conquering the Unknown

"How do I overcome my fears of the unknown?" may be on your mind right now. The solution is as easy as taking things one step at a time. Rely on your friends, family, and partner as your support system. They will serve as your rock and a sounding board for your troubles at odd hours.

Also, never forget that it's acceptable to request assistance when necessary. Seeking guidance or help doesn't make you a less competent parent; parenting is a team effort. It's a sign of knowledge and strength.

Why Have More Children?

You may find yourself thinking about growing your family while you and your first kid negotiate the exciting journey that is motherhood. Here's a secret: you might be craving more because of the happiness, love, and laughter your child brings into your life.

Every child is a unique work of art, and as your family grows, you get to witness the wonder of seeing them develop and learn about the world in a way that is uniquely their own. Not to mention the brotherly bond between siblings, where they play games together, share secrets, and, of course, fight over who gets the last cookie.

Thus, as you go out on this amazing journey that is parenthood, keep in mind that fear is normal, but don't let it stop you. Enjoy the laughing, embrace the unknown, and treasure every moment you have with your child. Who knows, maybe someday you'll be the one inspiring others to take on the wonderful journey that is parenthood. After all, the happiness that comes with having additional children can be the greatest adventure of them all!

Chapter 2

Key Steps To Creating An Irresistible Home For Your Children

When we were kids, we recall how our home environment had a significant influence on how we handled life on a daily basis until we were adults. The family environment that our parents created played a part in shaping who we are today. As you grow your children to become successful adults, the one thing you can completely control is creating a positive home environment for them.

I had the good fortune to grow up in a loving family where my parents supported and loved us unconditionally. I want to give my spouse and children that same happy feeling now that I'm a mother.

You see, kids who grow up in a cozy and supportive environment go on to become content and self-assured adults.

I have acquaintances who are also mothers who were raised in less-than-ideal circumstances. Being raised in a bad household appears to have had a permanent negative impact on their lives. They also made a different decision for the family they are now raising because they are aware of how it feels. They taught me that growing up in a dysfunctional household causes emotional harm. Your social skills develop in a way that makes life difficult for you every day. You'll embrace the relationships you witness at home as being part of your own. Anxiety and sadness stem from dysfunctional households.

Create the groundwork for a happy, future-focused household with these tried-and-true suggestions.

1. Make Every Day A Happy Return Home.

The door where you greet your loved ones each day is where happiness begins. More than just bidding them farewell, a warm and enthusiastic welcome affects their disposition.

When my husband gets home from work, I'll stop whatever I'm doing and tell the kids, "Dad is home!" The children immediately dash to the door, giving him big, kissing hugs. I have always enjoyed seeing this lovely sight repeatedly play out in front of my eyes as a mother.

We follow the same routine when my oldest child gets home from school. There's no exchanging of labor, assignments, or other unfinished business through that door.

2. Pick Proper Expressions and Words

Words like jerk, ugly, stupid, and stupid have no place in a happy home. Happiness begins at home, thus even though we have little control over what our children hear outside the house, such negativity should end there.

Our home is the secure haven for our family. We do not accept negativity here as much as possible. Sibling arguments are common, though, and they ought to be resolved over a milk and cookie snack. We make sure our children don't see parent-child arguments because it may influence how they perceive relationships.

Limit the kids' access to devices at home so that things like TV shows, unsupervised internet browsing, social media, or even music won't influence their language choices.

3. Show Them Love and Encouragement.

Some parents believe that in order to discipline their children, they must project a strict image. However, fear does not equate to deference. It's quite acceptable to show your children affection. In actuality, they require it now more than ever.

I feel like I can't even go a day without giving my guys a hug as a mother. One moment they might be two tiny devils, the next they might be the cutest angels. In either case, I give them the same level of affection since it serves as a constant reminder that my love is here to stay.

A mother's love has a lasting, unconditional warmth to it. They are aware that even after they start their own families, I will be there to assist them.

4. Prioritize Rest and Quality Time.

The world in which we currently live moves quickly. In order to improve their children's future, parents labor hard and study hard. We occasionally lose sight of how crucial relaxation is to maintaining a balanced and healthful existence.

My spouse and I each have our unique ways of unwinding after work. Naturally, we also take into account the pressure our young lads are under. They have a lot going on during the day, so we want our house to be a location where they can unwind and get ready for the next one.

Before supper, we always give them their own time. My oldest usually completes his schoolwork, but we also frequently sit down to spend valuable time together as a family.

5. Be The Model of Positive Relationships

Have you ever noticed how kids pick up on everything you do? They look up to you as role models because you are the adults in the family. They take after you in all you say and do, adopting it into their own lives. When you model positive behavior at home, your children will grow up to be courteous, self-assured, and compassionate young adults.

Our kids witness my spouse and I's undying love for one another every day. We make an effort to be self-assured grownups that our children look up to. They inspire us to face our shortcomings and transform into better versions of ourselves. This is the benefit that comes from having a happy home.

Hacks To Control Kids in Using Electronic Devices

We can officially say that electronic devices have taken over our lives and are not going away anytime soon. We always carry computers, iPads, TVs, and cell phones with us. For children ages two and younger, recommendations allow a maximum of two hours of digital screen usage. According to studies conducted in 2014, kids' favorite toys of the day are electronic gadgets. For leisure, half of all children spend more than four hours a day in front of an electronic gadget.

Tablets and laptops are examples of electronic gadgets that are necessary for academic study in schools. That being said, you shouldn't let your kids use these devices for longer than necessary because of this.

They may be wasting their time on pointless websites or games. Advocates of educational media technology refer to these endeavors as "empty calories." Similar to junk food, if parents don't set boundaries for both content and time, their kids may become addicted to this material.

There are several strategies to help kids quit their addiction to electronics.

1. Establish a public area in your house for personal use of tablets, laptops, and desktop computers. This is a method of limiting the amount of time that children have to themselves to play games and browse the internet.

They'll be more careful about the websites and games they visit if the whole family is nearby. Younger children attending preschool will need to be prohibited from using smaller electronic devices, such as cell phones. The decision of when to get your elementary school student a personal phone must be made.

2. Secure your personal electronics with a password. Youngsters ought to understand how to request permission. Furthermore, if you are aware of when your child uses your phone, you will know how much time and at what times they are spending on screens. It's also a good idea to set up passwords for the websites on the family laptop or computer to prevent your children from using your credit card to purchase in-game goodies.

3. Establish timetables and spare time. Establish a NO PHONES rule for your children at the dinner table. Tell them ahead of time if they need to put the device away and remind them when dinner is. For example, your child is still playing ten minutes before suppertime.

Acknowledge that their allotted time is almost over by acting as their timer. A child will throw tantrums if their games are forced to be put away on time, and this might develop into a dangerous habit later on.

4. Create a distraction. According to studies, children who are bored are more prone to become addicted to digital games and gadgets. Make sure your child has a fun-filled schedule for the entire day. Allocate more time for physical activities such as sports and less time for online entertainment. Nothing is more beneficial than helping your youngster develop their social skills.

5. You have to set an example for your children in whatever you teach them if you want them to listen to you. Bringing work home is often unavoidable, particularly during busy client seasons. On the other hand, keep your kids' access to your mobile and computer expenses restricted. Remember to abide by your "NO PHONE" rule when eating.

6. Some parents have been known to use their smartphones as pacifiers to keep their children quiet. Allowing toddlers to play games on your phone will quickly distract their attention when they cry or annoy you for no apparent reason. Parents need to get rid of this unhealthy practice. Look for alternatives to your children pestering you. Usually, all you have to do is wait for their outbursts to stop.

7. If everything else fails, you simply need to remind your kids that you are in charge. Above all, you are their parent and the only adult in the home. If you take away the technology they are using to play, they are helpless.

They will eventually realize that it is in their best interests.

To help your children get off those electronic devices, use gradual transitions and distraction strategies like sports and other enjoyable outdoor activities. Involving parents in their kids' screen time offers a chance to develop a relationship and teach them new things. Good media relationships will result from the family adopting responsible electronic usage practices.

Chapter 3

Developing Your Child's Social Communication Skills

The term "social communication," also known as pragmatics, describes how adults and children utilize language in social contexts. It talks about the abilities needed to have discussions and use language for communication.

Pragmatics is defined as the social language skills people use in everyday interactions. It essentially consists of how we say things, how we say them, how we utilize body language, and whether or not it is appropriate for the situation. It is an essential communication ability in which we convey our feelings, ideas, and thoughts.

Some situations call for the use of pragmatic language. Rather than the structure of language, it focuses on how we use language to interact with various individuals in various contexts. More precisely, pragmatics is the capacity to observe and interpret nonverbal signs from others while adhering to social norms.

There are three primary skills in social communication.

First among them is our language proficiency. This is the ability to utilize language to express a variety of emotions, including welcoming, informing, demanding, promising, and requesting.

The second capacity is linguistic flexibility. With this ability, a person may adapt their speech to the situation or the listener.

The third crucial component of effective social communication is the capacity to adhere to the "unspoken" norms of discourse and storytelling. This entails being aware of when you're about to speak, rotating speakers, and remaining on the subject. When the other person doesn't understand what is being said, the speaker can also discover alternative ways to express themselves because of this capacity. This ability includes making eye contact, using body language and facial expressions, and understanding how close to stand someone when conversing.

It's critical to instill in your youngster the ability to comprehend the person they are speaking with. Conversational rules vary from culture to culture, among cultures, and even within different families; therefore, your child needs to be able to interpret them while speaking with others from diverse backgrounds or cultures.

Guide on Enhancing Your Child's Social Communication Skills

Building social ties will be much aided by your child's acquisition of effective communication skills. Pragmatic language abilities are especially beneficial in educational settings because most curriculum-based activities need peer collaboration and communication.

As they get older, it is expected of them to be able to demonstrate proficiency in social communication, even though they might not know and adhere to all social norms at this point.

Sometimes kids have trouble remaining on topic, narrating stories in an unorganized manner, or taking over conversations and ignoring other people. Children occasionally behave in this manner, which is normal, but if they do so frequently or in an age-inappropriate manner, there may be cause for concern.

You can practice the following to assist your child in developing strong social communication skills:

1. Play pretend games with your kid. Involve other family members or plan a playdate with other kids so you may act out social scenarios such as going to a concert in the park, hosting a tea party, or visiting grandparents.

2. Write tales together. After that, you can assist your child in appropriately structuring their thinking. Create stories with this activity to show people how to act in social situations. You could write a story about going to the theater, for instance. After that, you can instruct your youngster on how to act appropriately during a play and how to watch it with grace.

3. Puppets and Miming. Use puppets to narrate a story. Another effective approach to employing mime, gestures, and facial expressions to convey anything is to play charades.

4. Games that require turns. Your child can learn to take turns by playing board games. It is also a fantastic approach to teach kids that having fun and playing decently is more important than winning and that it is acceptable to lose (a concept known as sportsmanship).

5. Work on your greetings. Show your kids how to properly welcome strangers, including street sweepers, building receptionists, teachers, and grandparents. Urge your child to greet and bid farewell to others in social situations.

6. Be considerate and courteous. Teach your child how to use language politely by using direct or indirect methods (e.g., they can say, "The volume is a bit loud," rather than, "Turn off the music!"). Please let's try lowering it.

Having pragmatic language skills can enable your child to behave appropriately by assisting them in understanding others in a range of settings. Talking to your child about how individuals can respond differently based on how they were talked to will help them understand the significance of knowing when and how to modify language to get the desired effect.

Your kids will need social communication skills as they grow up and learn how to navigate the world. They will encounter more interactions as they get older that call for specific behaviors. You must provide children with the appropriate manners so they may build enduring relationships with others.

Chapter 4

Disciplining with Love

Loving your child would be the first element in any recipe for effective child discipline. I recently saw this in action. I was with a mother who had four young boys, no older than five. Her patience and composure were amazing! She began by allowing them to be themselves. She let them get noisy, throw a ball at each other, and run about the house. Her expectations were appropriately set.

She was calm, patient, and loving in her discipline when there was a sort of altercation.

"Was that a good choice or a bad choice?" she asked her oldest child.

A bad decision, he said.

"What option would be better?" she asked.

He answered saying, "Not throw the ball in Samuel's face."

With an abundance of love, she exclaimed, ***"That's a great choice!"***

I disciplined my son in the same caring way she had that very night.

Convincing kids to follow instructions and providing them with loving guidance when they don't is one of the hardest things parents have to do.

Parenting experts assert that there are three main strategies parents employ to get their kids to comply: coercion, love withdrawal, and induction.

* Coercive parents try to impose their will on their children by using harsh or violent methods including beating, yelling, ordering, or degrading behavior. Even while these tactics typically result in compliance, studies reveal that parents who regularly employ them raise socially awkward, withdrawn, unplanned, violent, and morally immature children.

* When a parent exhibits love withdrawal, they express dissatisfaction and withhold their affectionate attention until the behavior improves. For instance, they might stop speaking to their child until she obeys. Studies on the efficacy of this method yield conflicting findings, but they do suggest that if disciplined in this manner repeatedly, a kid may experience excessive guilt.

* Reasoning with kids and explaining how their actions affect other people are aspects of induction.

It encourages desired behavior with persistence and tactful persuasion. Induction is a more beneficial kind of discipline than either love withdrawal or force. Children of induction-regular parents have more developed consciences, as well as being more socially adept, accountable, internally driven to make moral decisions, autonomous, self-assured, and goal-oriented.

But sometimes, more than convincing arguments are needed to gain acquiescence. Parents might feel the need to scream, threaten, or even ground their child during these moments. The preferable course of action is to invoke consequences. Children learn for themselves that particular behaviors result in certain outcomes when parents let them experience the immediate consequences of their decisions rather than protecting them from these consequences. Instead of penalizing the youngster, the focus is on teaching him. For instance, a child who wakes up late and misses the bus will learn a valuable lesson if they have to walk to school rather than take their parent's car. If a child doesn't gather up her dirty socks and place them in the hamper, she should bear the immediate consequence of her decision—that is, not having any clean socks to wear.

As a parent, you must establish upfront the reasonable repercussions that will ensue from a certain infraction. A kid who violates curfew, for instance, forfeits the family automobile for a set period. A child forfeits the opportunity to spend time with friends for a certain amount of time if they visit them without first alerting their parents. Parents are probably punishing their children more often than they are teaching them when there isn't a clear link between conduct and its consequences.

Consequences must be administered to lead and instruct success. A child's long-term welfare should be considered when administering discipline, along with love and compassionate concern. Rather than using punishment as an excuse to lash out or get retribution, parents should genuinely want to teach their kids the right values. Never confuse parental authority with the right to abuse or dictate. Should we feel that suffering our kids "for their good," we're most likely not in the correct frame of mind.

When their children misbehave, some parents demand severe punishment or set penalties right away. However, before choosing a punishment plan, it's critical to comprehend the causes of a child's misbehavior. A child may exhibit maladaptive behavior due to a medical condition that needs to be treated. A child may be acting out to get attention, satisfy an unmet need, or communicate anxiety or fear. Teens who assist a stranded driver may experience delays returning home after an evening activity. In these kinds of situations, it would usually be unproductive to respond with instant punishment or the assignment of penalties. Rather than just responding to their children's behavior, parents ought to make a serious effort to comprehend it. With comprehension, parents can be better teachers and enforce rules more successfully for their kids. Parents who are fully aware of the factors underlying misbehavior can also make plans to avoid possible issues.

Children frequently have an especially intense need to feel their parents' affection after receiving correction. Even in situations where they misbehave, children should know that they are still loved and cherished. As a follow-up to discipline, wise parents reassure their kids that they are loved and taken care of.

How about spanking? While there is conflicting data regarding the effectiveness of spanking, most professionals concur that there are better alternatives. Teen spanking has especially detrimental effects on the adolescent and the parent-teen bond. Removing privileges, assigning time outs, offering chances for repentance and reconciliation, or enforcing other penalties are better approaches.

In a nutshell, the ideal discipline approach reduces reprimands and stays away from harshness. A fine balance must be struck between appropriate strictness and unwavering acceptance and love. Good discipline is always applied in the framework of a caring parent-child bond.

These useful tips will help you discipline lovingly:

1. Remain calm.

Reprimand kids while you're cool and collected, not when you're agitated and irritated. If you find yourself on the verge of disciplining someone out of anger, pause, inhale deeply, and count to thirty. Alternatively, send your youngster to his room and retreat to your bedroom to gather your thoughts and assess the circumstances.

2. Before you punish your child, try to understand why they are acting out.

Is your kid misbehaving because she needs attention, is she just tired or restless? Perhaps it would be better to give him a nap or some extra time with you rather than punish him. Is your boy in the normal twos, threes, and teenage years of growing, when he is looking for freedom? How can you assist him in pursuing independence responsibly and safely? Is he bothered by anything in the surroundings? Maybe he did not do well on an exam, or he lost a beloved toy, or he fears the dark. it may be that your child was simply ignorant. If so, instruct him as opposed to punishing him.

3. Apply the consequences.

Children learn through consequences how their activities impact both their own and other people's lives. Not as effective as threats and badgering are consequences. They work particularly well if your kids participate in choosing which misbehavior should result in what penalties. As an illustration:

Many parents have a habit of asking their children the Who-What-Where-When questions before they leave the house: Who will you be hanging out with?

How are you going to proceed? Where are you going to be? When are you going to be home? They concur on the solutions. Any modifications to the plans require phone approval. If not, friend privileges are temporarily suspended.

The majority of parents give their kids chores, usually with the understanding that they would be completed before supper. You may ask them to go to their rooms until they comply if they refuse to perform their duties. They miss meals if they don't.

4. Seek out alternatives to physical punishment and spanking.

Taking away privileges (you won't be able to use the car for a week if you drive unsafely), highlighting the harm or suffering ("You made your sister so sad when you called her that," or "This has damaged my trust in you"), and demanding restitution (apologizing, trying to repair damaged property or injured relationships) are some of the options.

5. Never stop loving.

Make sure you obey instructions for discipline with kindness and compassion. Reassure your kids that you love them despite your disapproval of their actions. Show them that you have believe in them "We are not perfect. The next time, I'm sure you'll perform better."

While you don't have to defend your actions when disciplining your kids, you should spend some time explaining the reasoning behind the discipline if you want them to understand it. For instance, when we have dinner, my kids usually lean on their chairs. In addition to making me insane, what they're doing puts the seats in danger. So I said, "That could break the chair or break you," rather than shouting for not leaning back.

I'm letting them come up with their course of action by reminding them of the implications of their actions. I only made a warning about what might happen if they did tilt the chair back, not telling them not to.

6. Adhere to facts.

It's simple to use a few zingers when reprimanding our kids when we're upset with them. What aspect of shutting off the TV do you not understand? Does that make you feel in love? Respect will exist where love exists. When it comes to disciplining our kids, we may still treat them with respect, even though we are the ones in charge.

Just consider the embarrassing footage of moms screaming at their children that you may have seen. Indeed, the kids might be instilled with fear. Indeed, the moms' acts don't seem to reflect the love that surely lies behind them.

7. Give many hugs.

One of the most important aspects of loving discipline is showing physical affection outside of designated times. Hugs, cheek kisses, and back pats are examples of physical touch that can serve as a concrete reminder to your child of your love. And it will feel even more natural to wrap up your period of discipline with a comforting and reestablishing hug if you and your child have developed a tactile link.

Chapter 5

Nurturing Tomorrow's Innovators by Fostering Their Imagination and Creativity

In a world that is changing quickly, creativity and creative thinking are becoming more and more valuable abilities. We are crucial in helping our children develop these traits because we are their parents and other primary carers. It is essential to raise imaginative and creative-thinking youngsters and to provide them with useful tools to develop their creative minds since the world requires unique ideas.

Children's creativity is a complex and dynamic quality that includes a wide range of behavioral, emotional, and cognitive traits. It entails having the capacity to come up with fresh concepts, answers, and excellent sentences.

Creativity begins with imaginative thought. Creative kids frequently have vivid imaginations and the ability to imagine possibilities beyond the present moment. They might create imaginary worlds, pretend games, or fantasies.

Creative children are inherently curious and want to explore their surroundings. They genuinely want to know more about the world they live in, they seek out new experiences, and they ask questions.

Creative children have cognitive flexibility, which enables them to approach issues and circumstances from multiple perspectives. They are receptive to different viewpoints and prepared to give unusual concepts more thought.

Creative kids are great at fixing problems. They take a creative approach to problems and are open to trying out various fixes. They frequently see challenges as chances for imaginative investigation.

Artistic means of expression, including painting, drawing, dancing, music, and storytelling, appeal to a lot of creative kids. They express their feelings and ideas through various channels.

Divergent thinking, which is coming up with multiple ideas or answers to a single issue or problem, is a trait of creative kids. They welcome uncertainty and complexity.

Being creative frequently calls for perseverance and the ability to overcome challenges. Even in the face of failure, imaginative kids can demonstrate perseverance in pursuing their artistic goals.

Risk-taking is a necessary component of creativity. Even when there's a potential for failure, creative kids aren't afraid to take chances and try new things.

Creative children can communicate their feelings, ideas, and experiences through other creative mediums. This can facilitate self-discovery and catharsis.

Play and creativity frequently go hand in hand. Children who are creative and playful sometimes have a sense of humor. Play gives kids the freedom to experiment and discover.

Creative children can work with others and express their thoughts clearly. They might be adept at cooperating on group projects and sharing their artistic endeavors.

Creative children may be passionate about what they do. Their passions drive them from the inside out, and they take pleasure in the creative process.

Artistic children are frequently more aware of beauty and aesthetics in their surroundings. They might be attracted to music, painting, or other artistic mediums.

It's crucial to remember that every child's creativity will uniquely express itself and that each child's creative development will be influenced by their unique temperament, experiences, and opportunities for creative exploration.

A child's creativity needs to be nurtured and supported by creating an atmosphere that values experimentation, curiosity, and self-expression as well as by acknowledging and appreciating each child's creative interests and strengths.

Effective Methods for Fostering Creativity

1. Establish a Creative Environment: Set aside a room in your house for artistic expression and research. Use creatively stimulating materials and open-ended toys to promote unstructured play.

2. Promote Divergent Thinking: To promote critical thinking, pose open-ended questions with several possible responses. Honor and validate original concepts and solutions.

3. Set Screen Time Limits: Although technology has many advantages, too much screen time can inhibit creativity. Establish sensible boundaries.

4. Encourage Extracurricular Activities: enroll kids in artistically expressive programs like athletics, music courses, or art classes.

5. Promote Problem-Solving: Give kids tasks and riddles that call for original thinking to solve them. Instill in them the importance of perseverance and learning from errors.

6. Storytelling and Reading: Reading helps kids imagine new things and exposes them to a variety of worlds and concepts. Promote storytelling and give children the freedom to construct their own stories.

7. Introduce Them to Diverse Cultures: Educating kids about various cultures and customs extends their horizons and encourages empathy and ingenuity.

8. Transform Their Perspective on Failure: Show kids that failure is a chance for learning and progress rather than something to be feared. Tell tales of well-known entrepreneurs and inventors who encountered obstacles along the way.

9. Promote a Growth Mindset: Stress that aptitude and intelligence are something that can be acquired via work and education.

10. Show Off Your Creativity: Highlight your artistic passions and interests to show that creativity is a lifelong commitment. Take part in artistic endeavors with your kids to promote camaraderie and collaborative imagination.

11. Embrace Learning Show your children that you are curious about the world and that you enjoy learning by modeling these traits.

It takes time, encouragement, and commitment to raise imaginative and creatively minded kids. Parents and other carers may equip their kids to be the creative thinkers and problem solvers of the future by creating a loving atmosphere, encouraging problem-solving techniques, accepting failure as a necessary step on the path to greatness. Since innovative ideas are what propel advancement and progress, by doing this we help them grow personally and improve society as a whole.

Chapter 6

Knowing Your Child's Gifts

First and foremost, we should see our kids as God's ideal gifts.

Every child is unique, and parents must recognize this, thus it is our responsibility as parents to support each child in realizing their full potential. A child's best interests might not align with those of another.

Personal Training.

I've been teaching horses for decades, and I approach each horse as an individual rather than a group. Every horse I've ever trained has a unique potential and growth pattern. Some people learn quickly, while others learn more slowly.

I have to modify my approach to fit the needs and possibilities of each horse while establishing objectives that take into account their unique personalities and skill levels.

Continuing from here, I treat my kids the same way because they are special people with a variety of abilities.

The majority of educational systems group kids together based on their age, which often results in unending comparisons because many kids find it difficult to meet expectations.

Champions with Gifts.
We must treat our kids as unique little champions. They require encouragement to grow at their own pace as well as the freedom to do so. Individuals must possess the bravery to overcome their constraints.

Parents and teachers frequently place limits on children's potential, but I've found that they are much more capable than we think.

Control in Education.

As a parent who homeschools, I can accommodate each child's unique requirements and have complete control over every element of their education.

When my child is having difficulty with a math idea, for instance, we study that specific arithmetic issue for a week before moving on. We decided not to move on, thinking that the math problem would work itself out! In this manner, I ensure that my kids comprehend each idea completely before advancing.

Typically, during a growth spurt, my kids require an increase in sleep duration. When needed, I can keep an eye on them and allow them to sleep. Recall that kids often can't develop until they sleep, so getting enough sleep is crucial for their healthy growth.

Guidance from God.

You can frequently only learn what your child needs by engaging in deep prayer and connection with God. Never forget that God is going to lead you every step of the way. Ask Him to show you your child's needs, gifts, and talents.

I advise you to consider your child's educational plan as well as their developmental stage. Then, modify as necessary to suit their unique requirements. This, in my opinion, is the formula for producing happy, healthy, self-assured kids.

Since every child develops at a different rate, avoid constantly comparing them to other kids their same age. Likewise, avoid setting unrealistic expectations for your kids because these can only cause them to feel defeated, frustrated, and discouraged.

Individual Coaching.

Every athlete in the professional ranks of sports receives individualized training. To help them meet their demands and accomplish their objectives, they have a team of people who are training and developing them. Even in team sports, professional athletes are not necessarily trained in a collective setting. Usually, they receive individual training before being assembled as a group.

Look, Think, and Pray.

Having children is a great privilege, and we all want the best for them and for them to fulfill their potential. I advise you to examine how you are raising your kids and make the necessary changes to foster their uniqueness.

Never forget that God will lead the way at every turn. He will bless you and give you courage, direction, insight, and strength so that your kids can grow up to be the people God intended them to be.

God commands us to love, nurture, and instruct our children while providing them with the Bible. They can live out the rest of their lives as God's disciples in this way.

Recall that having successful, contented children is a journey that should be appreciated as much as it is accepted.

Declaration.

This is a fantastic declaration that your child can make every day.

I am yoked to Jesus, so I can handle whatever that comes my way today. I will not be overcome when I give Him my worries because He will take care of me and bear my burden. Since God is the author and finisher of my faith, I therefore vow that today will not bring me down! I ask this In the name of Jesus, Amen.!

Other Books Written By This Author

How To Love A Narcissist: Guide to Navigating Relationships With Empathy And Boundaries

How To Get It Done: Master Self-Reflection, Break Negative Cycles, and Cultivate Relationship Bliss

How to Stay Young: Science-Based Guide for Enhancing Health as You Age.

Balancing Motherhood: A Guide to Finding Happiness, Nurturing Children, and Flourishing Together

WORKBOOK GUIDE FOR WOMEN WITH ADHD: Harness Your Strength, Improve Your Relationships, Manage Your Emotions, and Achieve Success

ADHD PARENTING GUIDE FOR TEEN KIDS: Advantage strategic Keys for raising kids with ADHD.

www.ingramcontent.com/pod-product-compliance
Lightning Source LLC
Chambersburg PA
CBHW071105260726
48661CB00006B/2466